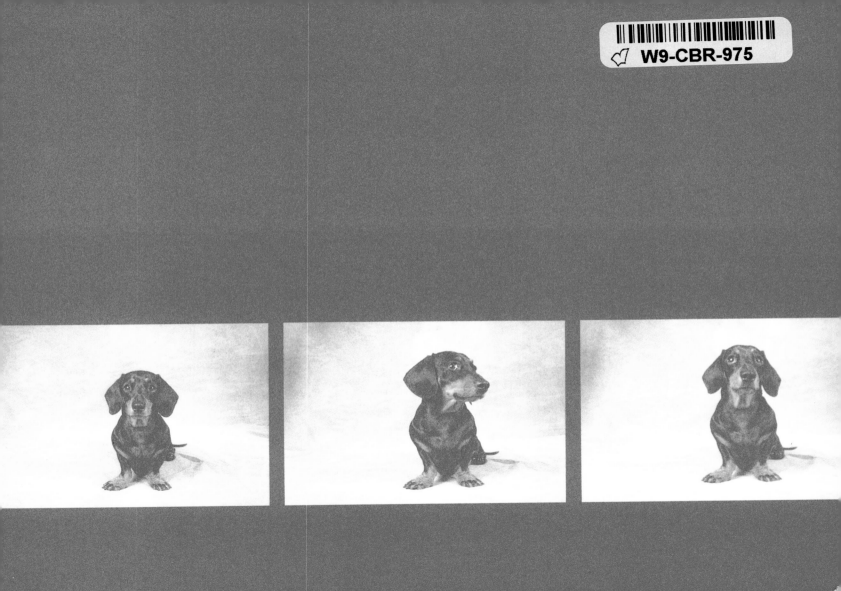

day of the
dachshund

day of the

dach

shund

jim dratfield

clarkson potter/publishers
new york

to dr. d and the psycho 5
for their dogged devotion to one another.

els 'n' dox

chowhounds

lunch dox

doggie bag

barking at the waiter

barking up the wrong tree

pooch 'n boots

pair-a-dox

pair-a-dox

devil dog

leashed

unleashed

dog training

scent in the hounds

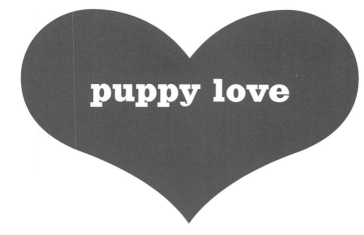

snout with clout

checked

mates

woofer 'n' tweeter

stoop

doggy dog

what's up, dox?

tongue

'n cheek

the dog in art

the dog out of art

sittin' on the dox of the bay

stretch . . . marks

paddle

links

on the links

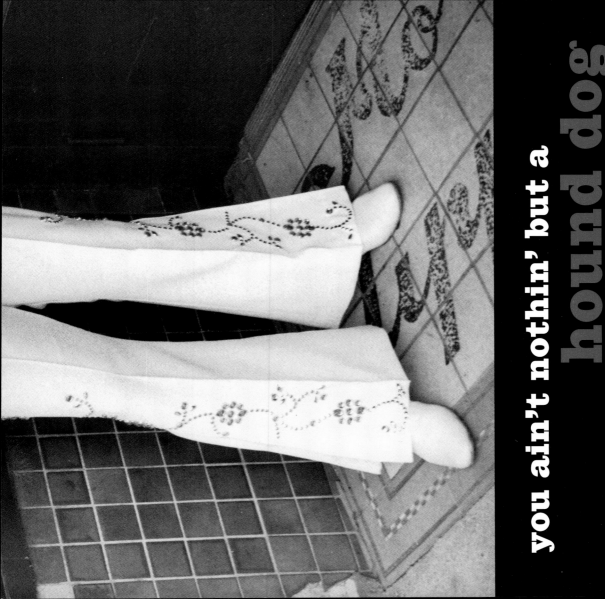

you ain't nothin' but a hound dog

by a hare

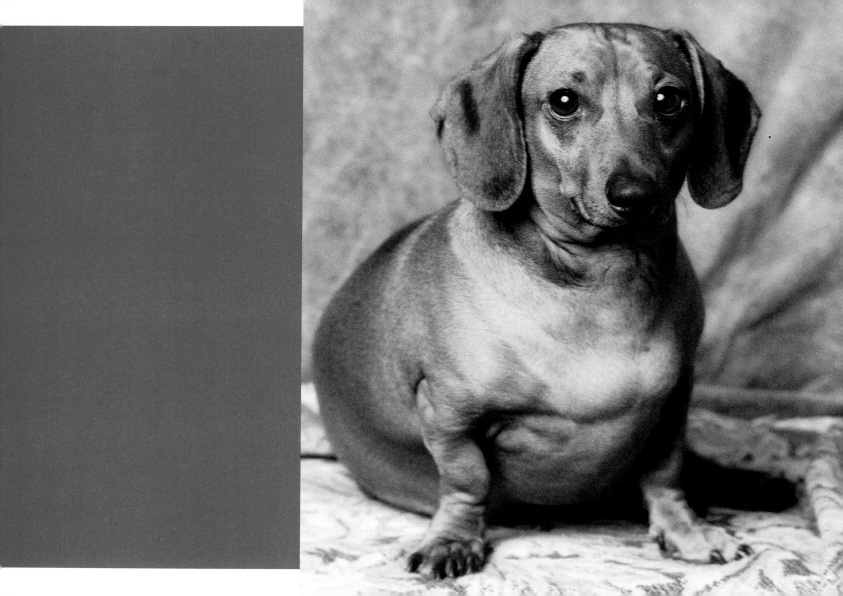

heavy petting

dog-**eared**

the eyes have it

sheep/dog

hang dog

dog days

of summer

dogma

pack o' dogs

a pup o' tea

got milk . . .

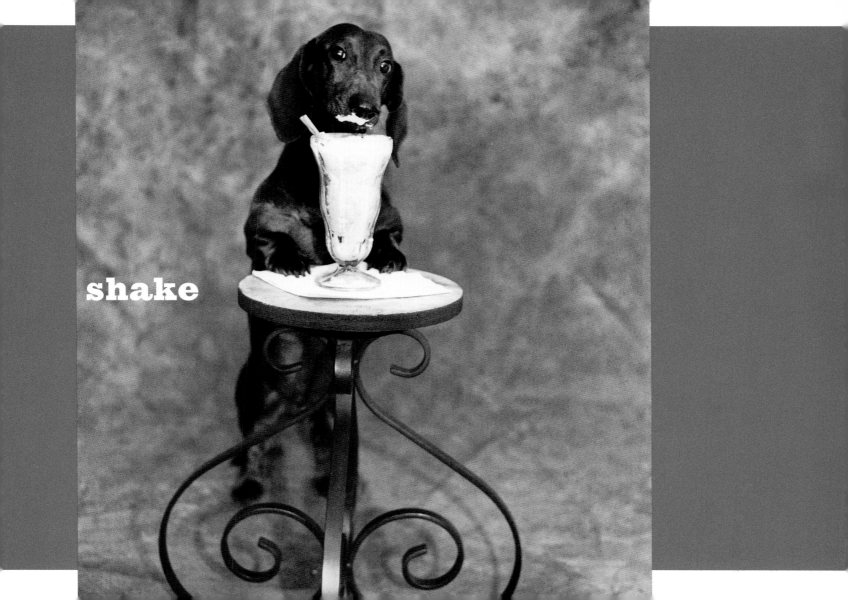

shake

baby **sit**   dog **sit**

dog **stand**

let sleeping dogs lie

hollywood

hound

hounded by guilt

hip hop

doxie with moxie

kosher hot dog

chilly dog

indoxicated

dog **doggone**

dox 'n' found

and the wiener is . . .

acknowledgments

First off, a thank-you to the wonderful team at Clarkson Potter, including Jane Treuhaft, Trisha Howell, and Linnea Knollmueller, who have continued to enhance my imagery with such keen production and design elements.

I must thank my editor, Chris Pavone, for continuing to steer our joint projects with great flair and panache. Kudos to Adina Steiman for making sure all goes ever so smoothly and without a hitch.

To Daniel Greenberg and those folks at the Levine-Greenberg Agency who not only watch over my career with great deftness, but add that intangible human touch to their efforts, as well. Dan, I always enjoy our chats over lunch.

I must offer a special thanks to Adrian and the Dachshund Friendship Club for their help and participation in this project.

To Dikerdachs for allowing me to include their wonderful dachshunds.

I had a "doggone" good time shooting portions of this book in Memphis and Germantown, Tennessee. Thank you to Amanda Wall for initiating the visit, and warmest affection to Nancy Barrow and all of those wonderful people and pooches involved with the Weenie Run. To Danny Spinosa of www.memphiselvis.com—you are truly the king of Elvis. To Don and Mary Scholund for loaning their boot to the cause and to Lisa Fortin for being such a gracious Graceland hostess.

To Heather for helping me with rounding up such gems of doxies for the L.A. shoots. To Elaine Seamans, Teri Austin, and the Amanda Foundation, whose love and concern for animals is second to none: I offer a thank-you for your help and support. To Tail O' the Pup for their good-natured patience with me while shooting at their historical establishment.

A thank-you must go out to each of the humans who were willing to travel near and far to allow me to capture their precious dachshunds on film for this book.

My last thank-you goes to all of the dogs on these pages, who humbled me with their character and their unique beauty, a group with an incredible variety of sizes, shapes, coats, temperaments, and personalities. To all of you dachshunds, I offer a final howl of appreciation!

Jim Dratfield is the photographer/owner of Petography (www.petography.com), which travels the country to photograph pets and their parents. He is the author of <u>Underdogs</u>, <u>The Quotable Equine</u>, and <u>Pug Shots</u>, and coauthor of <u>The Quotable Canine</u> and <u>The Quotable Feline</u>. Jim grew up in Princeton, New Jersey, and spent more than a decade acting on stage and the small screen. He now lives in New York City with his dog, Caleb.